HOLIDAY FUN

the date on w...
falls. If your days add up, you'll discover which year in the 1700s marked the first United States holiday established by Presidential proclamation. Perform each function as you move from top to bottom.

Halloween
(October)
+
Christmas
(December)
÷
Independence Day
(July)
+
Valentine's Day
(February)
+
St. Patrick's Day
(March)
x
Groundhog Day
(February)
−
New Year's Day
(January)
= 17__ __

Illustration: Diana Zourelias

Answer on page 48

SAILING SUMS

It's time for the regatta. Each yacht must sail around the buoys that are the same color as the boat's hull in order

to score points. The yacht with the highest score wins. Can you tell which ship will sail to victory?

Illustration: Bill Colrus

Answer on page 48

LOCKER LOGIC

Zelda just got a new locker. To help remember the combination, she put the numbers she needs at the end of some number sequences. Can you write the correct number and direction at the end of each line so that Zelda can get her sneakers in time for gym?

Illustration: R. Michael Palan

Answer on page 48

SWING SHIFT

There are 21 children waiting to swing on these three swings. Each child is allowed to swing for 10 minutes. If the first three children who are waiting start swinging at 1:00 p.m., what time will the last three children start swinging?

Answer on page 48

Illustration: Anni Matsick

HORSING AROUND

Even Steven and Odd Rod are two Pony Express riders who are racing through the Blocky Mountains. But while they're working, they like to have a little fun. Follow the path from the riders outward. If the answer to an equation is

Illustration: Rick Geary

an even number, write the letter below it under Steven's name in the order you found it. If the answer is odd, write the letter under Rod's name. If you use your horse sense, you'll be able to find the messages they're carrying.

Even Steven:

__ __ __ __   __ __   __ __ __   __ __ __ __

__   __ __ __ __   __ __ __ __ __ __ __ __ ?

Odd Rod:

__   __ __ __ __ __   __ __   __

__ __ __ __ __ __ __ __ __   __ __ __ __ __

Answer on page 48

KEY CLUES

Find the answer to each description. For extra help, the letter in the box will appear somewhere in the next answer. When you're finished, see if you know what all these words have in common.

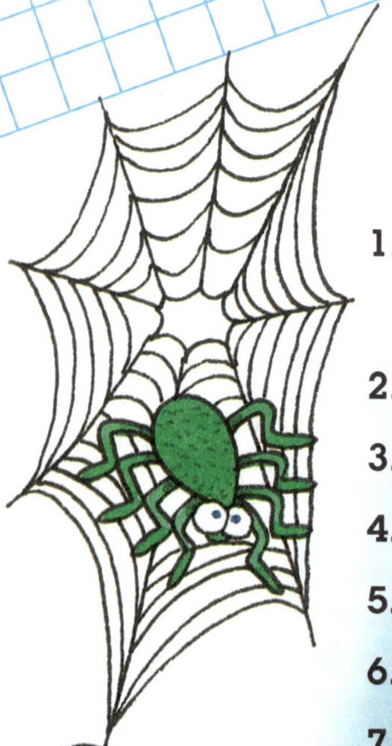

1. A small amount, or the part of the rein that goes in a horse's mouth: ___ ___ [ ]
2. Cowboy footwear: [ ] ___ ___ ___
3. Insect: ___ [ ] ___
4. To ride a board on wavy water: [ ] ___ ___ ___
5. Small, quiet rodent: [ ] ___ ___ ___ ___
6. Male sheep: [ ] ___ ___
7. Cold-causing germ: ___ [ ] ___ ___ ___
8. Crunchy potato snack: ___ ___ [ ] ___
9. Glass panes in your walls: [ ] ___ ___ ___ ___ ___ ___
10. Spider's home: ___ [ ] ___
11. Restaurant's food list: ___ ___ [ ] ___
12. Wire mesh that lets a breeze through a window: ___ ___ ___ ___ ___ ___

Hint on page 46

Illustration: Don Robison

Answer on page 48

DOTS A LOT

Join these even numbers to find a place to have a good time.

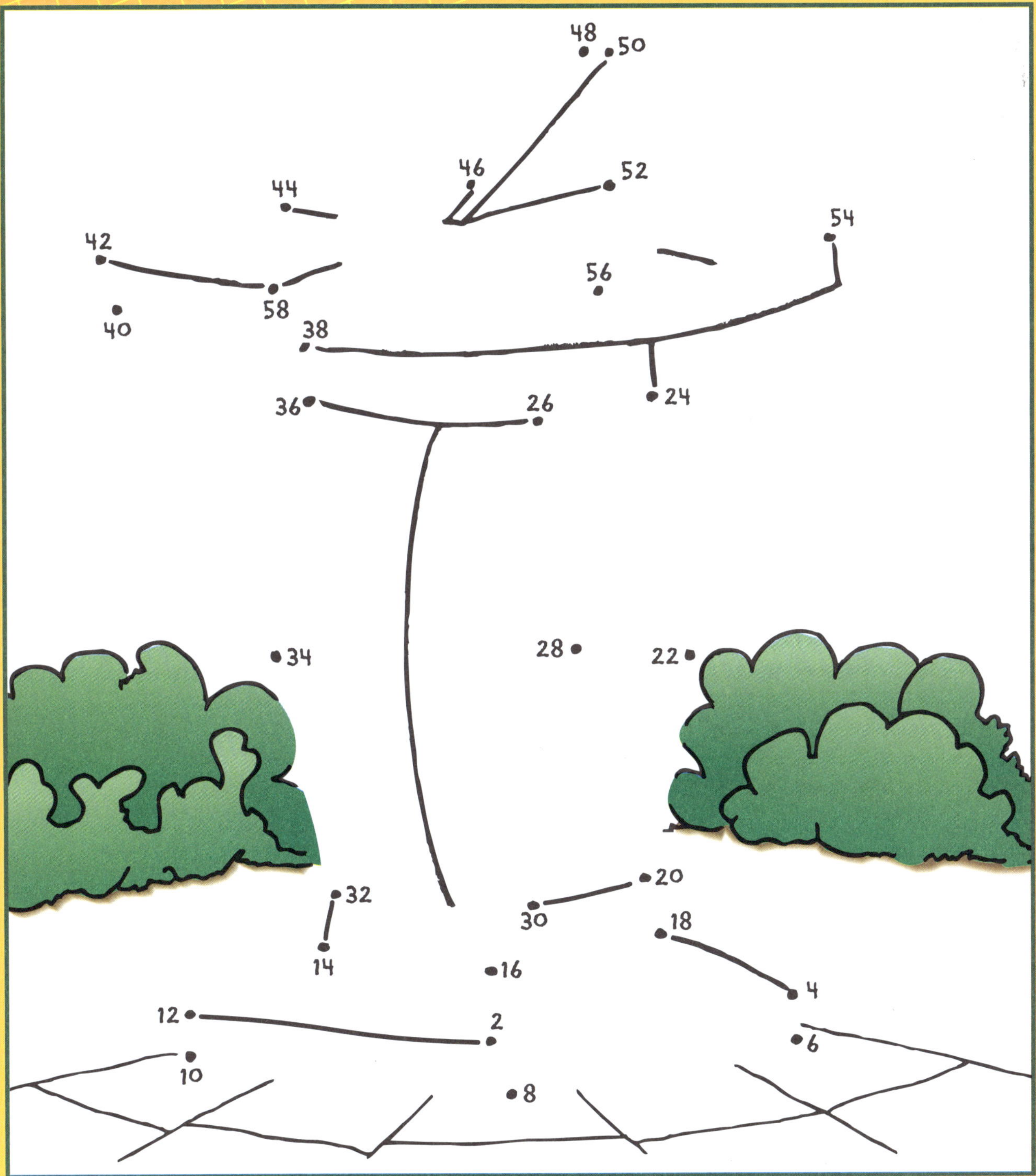

Illustration: John Puntar

Answer on page 48

FLIGHT TIMES

Can you help answer the questions for these people who are waiting for passengers to arrive?

1. Alan's flying from Athens. What gate will he arrive at?
2. Candy's coming from Cairo. What flight will she be on?
3. Leanne is traveling from London. What time will she actually get in?
4. How late is Danny's flight from Dublin?
5. Mischa's flight from Moscow was to come in at gate 8. At which gate is it scheduled to arrive now?
6. Will any flights arrive on time today?
7. Will any flights arrive early?
8. Which plane is delayed the longest?
9. Which late plane will come in closest to its expected arrival time?
10. Which flight has the lowest flight number?
11. How late is the flight from Sydney?

Flight #	Arriving From	Time Due	Actual Arrival	Arrival Gate
529	Rio de Janeiro	2:00 a.m.	1:00 p.m.	2
651	Boston	6:40 a.m.	7:05 a.m.	9
497	Fargo	7:12 a.m.	9:20 a.m.	4
511	Dublin	8:30 a.m.	8:35 a.m.	11
9450	Moscow	9:15 a.m.	9:35 a.m.	7
1402	Tokyo	10:00 a.m.	10:00 a.m.	10
739	London	11:15 a.m.	11:45 a.m.	12
222	Cairo	11:40 a.m.	12:05 p.m.	3
1006	Sydney	12:00 a.m.	12:15 p.m.	5
315	New York	12:33 p.m.	12:18 p.m.	6
8	Athens	1:50 p.m.	1:40 p.m.	1
477	Vancouver	3:10 p.m.	12:05 a.m.	8

Hint on page 46

Illustration: Rocky Fuller

Answer on page 48

STACKING STANLEY

A big sale on triangles is going on this week, and Stan needs to stock this shelf. He's got room for 10 triangles across. And he can stack others on top of that row. But is there any way he'll ever be able to fit a total of 38 triangles here?

Hint on page 46

Illustration: R. Michael Palan

Answer on page 48

THINK ABOUT IT

See how you fare against these number teasers.

Illustration: Jerry Zimmerman

1. What number becomes nothing when you add one letter to it?

2. What number sounds as if it has already eaten?

3. Why were the other numbers afraid of 7?

4. Only one number has the same number of letters in it as the number it is. Which number?

Answer on page 48

CARNIVAL CLUES

Five friends went to the carnival. Each rode his or her favorite ride a number of times. From the clues here, can you tell who rode which ride and how many times each child rode?

Answer on page 49

	Roller coaster	Teacups	Ferris wheel	Fun house	Train	Number of Times				
Antonia										
Beryl										
Delia										
Carlos										
Edward										

Use the chart to help you. The children are listed, as well as the names of their rides. When you find information that matches, put a circle where the columns and rows meet. Put an X in the rest of the row in that section.

Illustration: Michael Austin

- A boy rode the train.
- No one rode more than eight times.
- No two children rode the same number of times.
- Antonia rode the roller coaster half as many times as Delia went on her ride.
- Edward rode his ride twice as many times as Beryl rode hers.
- Beryl rode one time fewer than Antonia.
- Beryl doesn't like the fun house.
- Carlos rode the ride that comes first alphabetically.
- Delia rode her ride the most.
- Carlos rode one time more than Edward.

Hint on page 46

COUNTING PLACES

Each country contains letters that spell out a number from 1 to 10. Most letters are scattered in each word and do not appear in order. Can you find one number hiding in each country that doesn't appear in any other country?

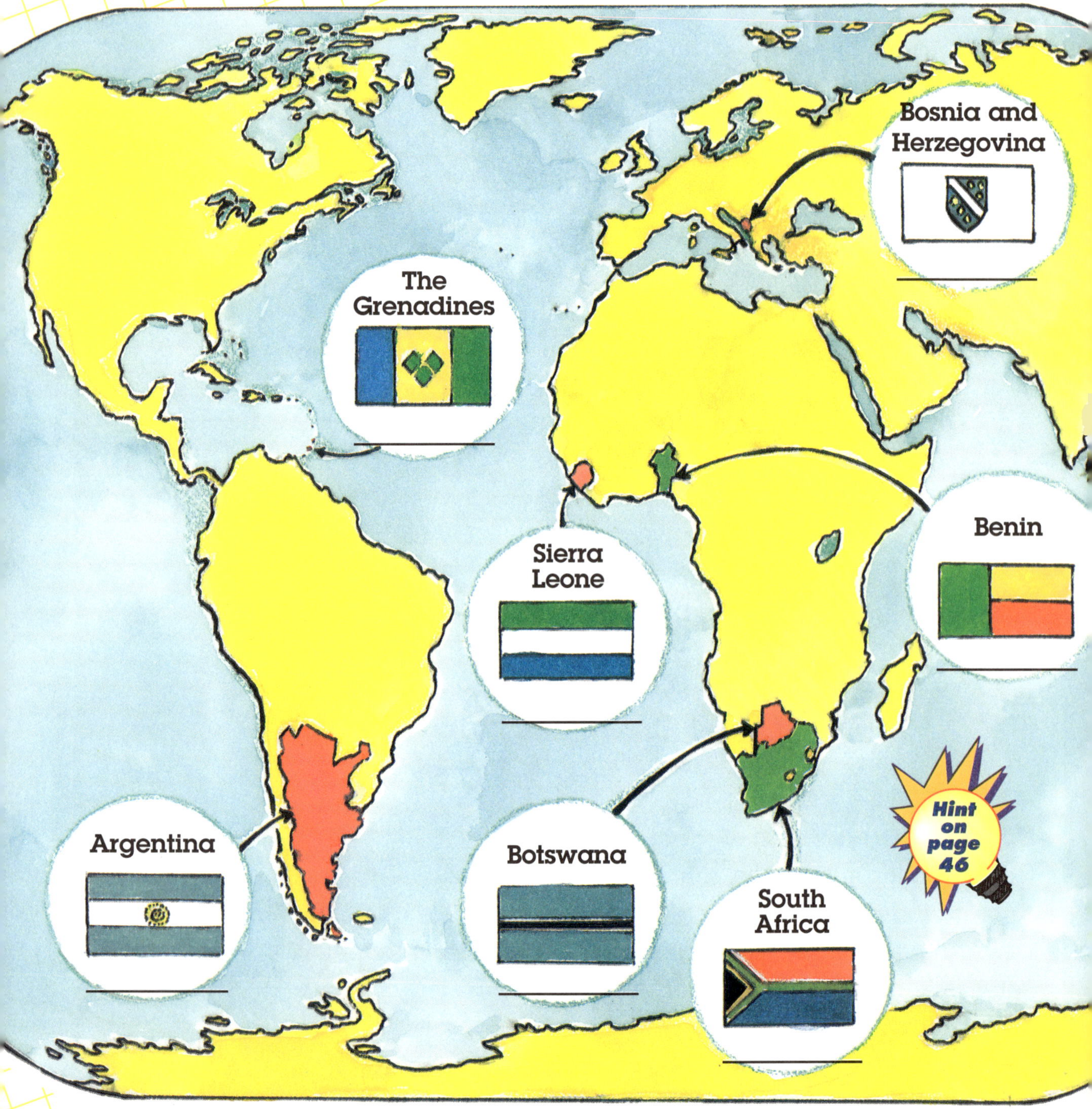

Illustration: Marc Nadel

Answer on page 49

FAST TIMES

Can you come up with some fast answers for these multiplication problems?

A $25 \times 20 \times 31 \times 0 \times 10 = ?$

B $6{,}718{,}923 \times 1 = ?$

C $5{,}000{,}000 \times 2 = ?$

Hint on page 46

Answer on page 49

CROSSNUMBER

Answer each question as you would in a regular crossword, and then place the numbers into the grid, one number per box.

ACROSS

1. The year Christopher Columbus made his first voyage to the New World
4. Many believe this number is unlucky.
6. The decimal system is based on this number.
7. February tenth
9. A picture is said to be worth this many words.
10. A quarter of something is this percent.
12. The last date of any year
14. Last year of the 19th century
16. 1 ton minus 10 pounds
17. Number of thieves who went against Ali Baba
18. Number of feet in 10 yards
19. Translate these Spanish numbers: *cero, dos, cinco, tres*

DOWN

1. Next two numbers in this sequence: 3, 4, 7, 8, ?, ?
2. Number of days it rained on Noah
3. 1,000,000 doubled
4. Number in this time: three minutes after eleven
5. Number of days in September
8. Objects in a score
11. $100.00 - $48.10
13. Year the Wright brothers took flight
15. 100-1
16. Number of original colonies
17. Number of minutes in $\frac{3}{4}$ of an hour

Illustration: Rick Geary

Answer on page 49

THREE BEES

Four rows are here, but the object is to make sets of three. Pick one word in each column that belongs in the same category. For example, *SINGLE, DOUBLE,* and *TRIPLE* go together. Now see if you can pick the words for three other groups and write each group in a row.

SINGLE	TWO	THREE
ONE	SECONDARY	THIRD
FIRST	DOUBLE	TERTIARY
PRIMARY	SECOND	TRIPLE

SINGLE	DOUBLE	TRIPLE

Answer on page 49

Illustration: David Helton

MAIL RUN

This mail truck will visit each mailbox only once and then return to the starting point. We've already delivered part of the path. You can move across or up and down, but not diagonally. Can you find the rest of the way?

START

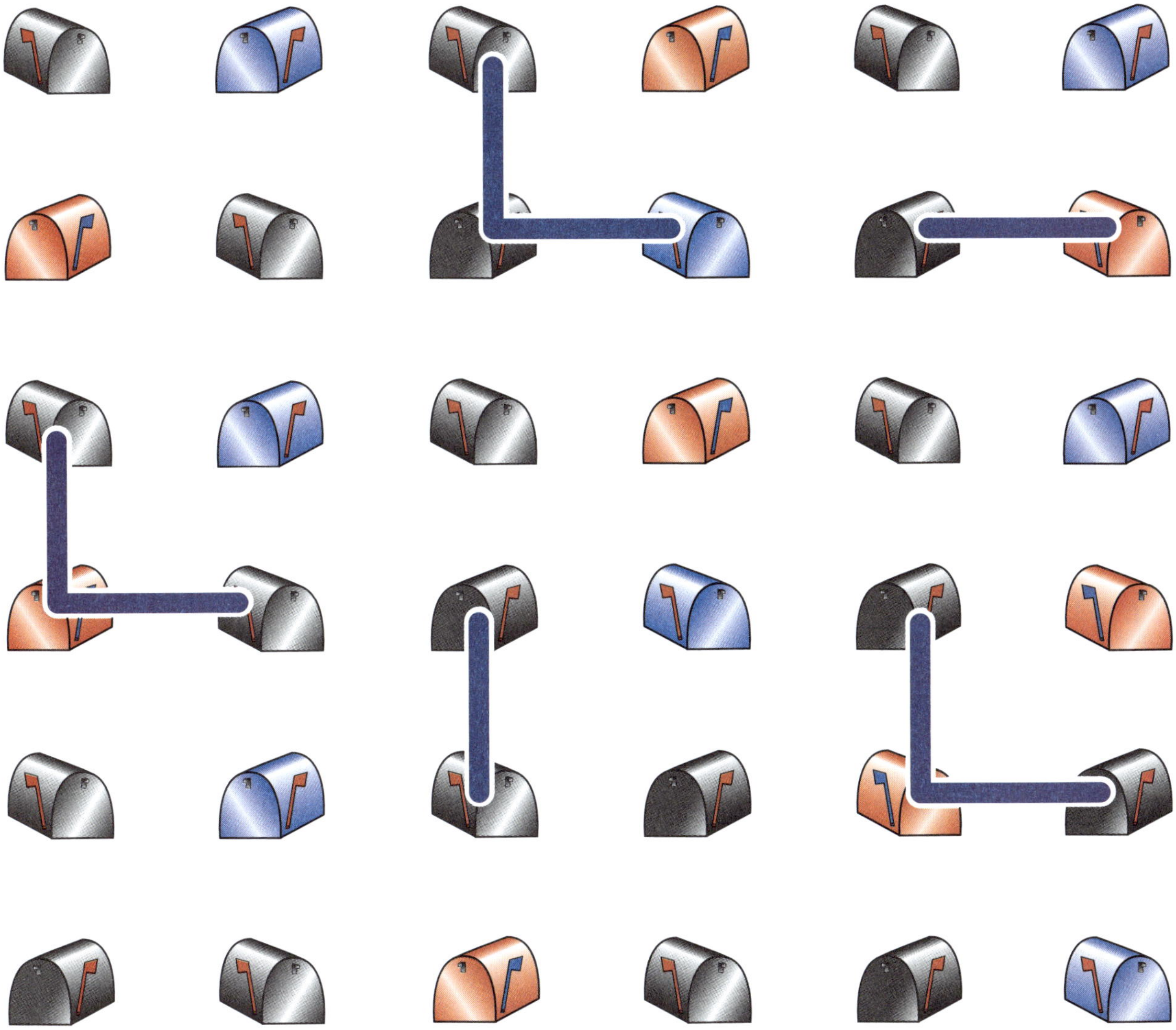

Answer on page 49

DIGIT DOES IT

The buzz in Inspector Digit's neighborhood is not good. Something has upset the delicate balance of the quiet suburban life. A neighbor's note should provide

Answer on page 49

a clue about what's going on. Can you help the Inspector decipher the cryptic clue so he can get in on a real "sting" operation?

5 6 2 17 10 14 18 16 6 4 19 15 17 5 10 8 10 19,

22 15 20 17 5 15 8 11 14 15 4 11 6 5

15 21 6 17 13 22 2 16 10 2 17 10 6 18!

13 22 3 6 6 18 1 6 17 6 9 10 21 6 12 6 18 18.

2 7 6 1 1 15 17 11 6 17 18 2 17 6

18 19 10 12 12 13 10 18 18 10 14 8. 10 1 15 14 ' 19

5 17 15 14 6 15 14' 3 20 19 1 15 20 12 5

12 10 11 6 22 15 20 17 9 6 12 16 19 15

7 10 14 5 13 22 12 2 18 19 A B 3 6 6 18.

9 15 14 6 22 3. 3 20 13 3 12 6

Hint on page 47

Illustration: John Nez

SCRAMBLED PICTURE

Copy these mixed-up rectangles onto the next page to unscramble this picture.

The letters and numbers tell you where each rectangle belongs. The first one, A-3, has been done for you.

Illustration: Rob Sepanak

Answer on page 49

JUST A SECOND

Take a moment to fill in all these answers that include the word *second*. To help you, the answers follow in alphabetical order.

1. Place to go if you hit a double: second ______________
2. To come up short, miss first place: second ______________
3. An opportunity to try again: second ______________
4. The son or daughter of your aunt's son or daughter: second ______________
5. Type of burn that causes blisters: second-______________
6. To serve underneath someone; sounds like a musical instrument: second ______________
7. The level above the ground in a building: second ______________
8. To have doubts about your first answer: second-______________
9. Once owned by someone else: second______________
10. Something done by instinct, without thinking: second ______________
11. Advice from an additional doctor: second ______________
12. To see into the future: second ______________
13. Come up with a better idea after already starting something: second ______________
14. Renewed energy after a short rest: second ______________

Illustration: Don Robison

Hint on page 47

Answer on page 49

FAMILY LOGIC

1. Among their children, Mr. and Mrs. Numerator have seven boys. Each boy has two sisters. How many children are in the Numerator family?

Hint on page 47

Illustration: Jerry Zimmerman

2. In the Denominator family, all the children have either red hair or brown hair. Each red-haired child has the same number of red-haired siblings as brown-haired ones. But each brown-haired child has twice as many red-haired siblings as brown-haired ones. How many children are in the Denominator family?

Answer on page 50

PIPELINES

This one is "plumb" tough. Can you join all of these pipes together so that the water can get from the reservoir to the houses? The ends of the pipes that equal the same number will fit together.

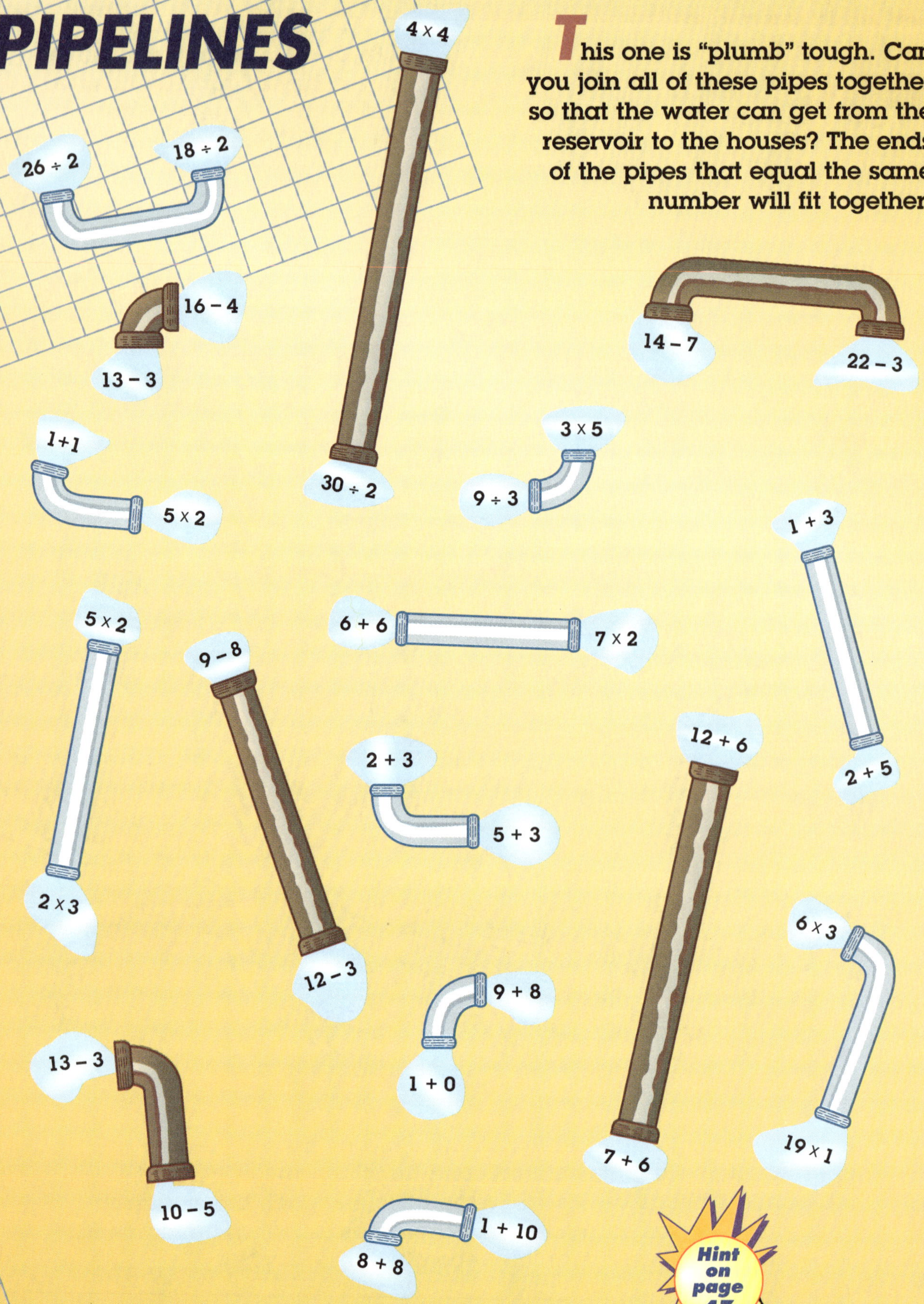

Hint on page 47

Illustration: Jason Thorne

Once you figure out which pipes connect, draw them into the right spots to show the layout of the pipes.

Answer on page 50

MATHMAGIC

Illustration: Marc Nadel

SAND ART

Can you trace this design without going back along or crossing over any lines?

Illustration: Barbara Gray

Answer on page 50

TO A DISTANT PLANET

These four rocket jockeys are setting out to fly from their space station to four different planets. Each captain will fly to the planet that matches the color of his, her, or its ship. Count each star along their paths to find the distance.

Capt. Spiff Daring
Count each star along the path. Multiply that number by 1,000 to find the number of miles.

Capt. Quixocort
Count each star along the path. Multiply that number by 5,280,000 to find the number of feet traveled. Capt. Quixocort will still need to compute the miles.

Then help each captain convert the journey to miles. Can you tell who will have the longest flight? You may want to use a calculator for this puzzle—unless you have an in-flight directional-distance triangulation scanner like the captains have.

Hint on page 47

Illustration: Michael Austin

Answer on page 50

Capt. Bruce Baxter
Count each star along the path. Multiply that number by 2,299 to find the number of kilometers traveled. Capt. Baxter will still need to compute the miles.

Capt. Manga Conn
Count each star along the path. Multiply that number by 1,936,000 to find the number of yards traveled. Capt. Conn will still need to compute the miles.

LIBRARY LAUGHS

Dewey has some funny books in his library. To check one out, solve each problem. Then go to the shelves to find the volume with the number that matches each answer. Put the matching letter in the blank beside each answer. Read down the letters you've filled in to find the title and author of the book Dewey just finished reading.

5 + 3 = ___ ___
3 x 5 = ___ ___
29 – 6 = ___ ___
27 ÷ 3 = ___ ___
4 + 3 = ___ ___
7 ÷ 7 = ___ ___
24 – 4 = ___ ___
4 x 2 = ___ ___
3 + 2 = ___ ___
27 – 9 = ___ ___
40 ÷ 8 = ___ ___
2 x 2 = ___ ___
9 ÷ 3 = ___ ___
6 x 3 = ___ ___
18 – 3 = ___ ___
13 + 3 = ___ ___
16 + 3 = ___ ___
8 – 6 = ___ ___
5 x 5 = ___ ___
36 ÷ 2 = ___ ___
12 – 11 = ___ ___
8 + 6 = ___ ___
12 ÷ 3 = ___ ___
5 x 5 = ___ ___
14 + 6 = ___ ___
2 x 9 = ___ ___
9 – 8 = ___ ___
45 ÷ 15 = ___ ___
14 + 6 = ___ ___
29 – 14 = ___ ___
11 + 7 = ___ ___

Hint on page 47

Answer on page 50

PIE TIME

To raise funds, the Ladies Auxiliary is selling pies by the slice. But anyone who can put these slices together into three different pies gets to keep one pie. Can you do it?

Illustration: Vilma Ortiz-Dillon

Answer on page 50

HOWARD'S HOUSE

Howard is having a big party. In order to attend, you need to figure out which house is his.

Read the directions on his invitation and see if you can find Howard's house.

1. My house is red.
2. My house has a porch.
3. My house is between two houses with flower gardens in the front yard.
4. My house has an even number.
5. You can divide my house number by 5.
6. My house number is a multiple of 8.

Illustration: Diana Zourelias

Answer on page 50

SIMONE SAYS

Simone has four little pieces. She needs to fit them in the big shape on the table. Can you arrange the four pieces into one?

Illustration: R. Michael Palan

Answer on page 51

COLOR BY NUMBERS

1 dot—Yellow
2 dots—Red
3 dots—White
4 dots—Light blue
5 dots—Dark blue
6 dots—Green

Color each shape here, using the chart as a guide.

Illustration: Rob Sepanak

Answer on page 51

ANIMAL AIRLIFT

The flood waters are up on the Watchout River. The Animal Association wants to move all the animals before the water gets too high. The helicopter can only hold up to 1,000 pounds of animals at any one time.

Answer on page 51

So for example, the helicopter can't take the elephant and the hippopotamus in one trip because they weigh too much when flown together. Can you figure out the fewest number of trips needed to move all the animals to a safe location?

Hint on page 47

FILL IT UP

This water spout is so rusted that it can't be turned on or off. However, Jenny knows it drips 8 ounces in a minute. Can you tell how long it will take to fill each of the measures Jenny has here?

Hint on page 47

Illustration: R. Michael Palan

Answer on page 51

CLOCK WATCHERS

Can you answer these questions in a timely manner?

1. Last night you went to bed at 9:30. Luckily, you can sleep late, so you set the wind-up alarm for 10:00 in the morning. How much sleep did you get?

2. One hour ago, it was as long after 1:00 in the afternoon as it was before 1:00 in the morning. What time is it now?

Illustration: Bill Colrus

3. Can you make two straight lines across the face of this watch, dividing it into three parts, so that the numbers in each part add up to 26?

Answer on page 51

HINTS AND BRIGHT IDEAS

These hints may help with some of the trickier puzzles.

COVER

One easy way to find the answer is to first add all the numbers together. Then check your total.

LOCKER LOGIC (page 6)

Look for a sequence in both number and direction.

KEY CLUES (page 10)

The boxed letter is there only as a clue to give you one letter in the next word. Don't let it throw you off.

FLIGHT TIMES (pages 12-13)

The time 12:00 a.m. is considered noon.

STACKING STANLEY (page 14)

If Stan turns a triangle in a new direction, he might get the point.

CARNIVAL CLUES (pages 16-17)

Antonia rode the roller coaster four times.

COUNTING PLACES (page 18)

The spelled-out numbers are 1, 2, 4, 7, 8, 9, and 10.

FAST TIMES (page 19)

These equations look a lot harder than they really are. Look for the smallest number in each and go from there.

CROSSNUMBER (pages 20-21)

The Wright year is 1903. When trying to find a quarter of anything, think how much a quarter is worth. When writing out a month that comes before October, 0 is always the first number. So February tenth would be 0210.

DIGIT DOES IT **(pages 24-25)**

The word *Inspector* appears in the note's greeting. Use the code numbers from this word to help figure out the rest of the message.

JUST A SECOND **(page 28)**

You'll have the *best chance* of making a good *guess* if you use the information at *hand.*

FAMILY LOGIC **(page 29)**

You're looking for the lowest possible number in each case. The Denominator clan has one more red-haired child than brown-haired one.

PIPELINES **(pages 30-31)**

First find the pipe ends that have the same answer. Those are your connections. Then draw how you think the pipes should look on the blueprint.

TO A DISTANT PLANET **(pages 34-35)**

Each mile consists of 5,280 feet or 1,760 yards or 1.6093 kilometers.

LIBRARY LAUGHS **(page 36)**

Remember to consult the books to find the letter that matches each number.

PIE TIME **(page 37)**

Each whole pie is made of slices from three different pies.

SIMONE SAYS **(page 40)**

Draw the figures on paper and cut them out. Then move them around to create one big design.

ANIMAL AIRLIFT **(pages 42-43)**

One flight out will take four animals. Another flight will take only two.

FILL IT UP **(page 44)**

There are 8 ounces in a cup, 2 cups in a pint, 2 pints in a quart, and 4 quarts in a gallon.

ANSWERS

COVER
Car 17 will win.

HOLIDAY FUN (page 3)
31 + 25 ÷ 4 + 14 + 17 × 2 – 1 = 89. In 1789, George Washington declared November 26 a day of national thanksgiving.

SAILING SUMS (pages 4-5)

White	7 + 3 + 9 + 2 + 1 + 9 = 31
Purple	6 + 5 + 8 + 3 + 2 + 4 = 28
Green	5 + 7 + 9 + 3 + 6 + 4 = 34
Red	2 + 5 + 9 + 1 + 6 + 3 = 26
Yellow	3 + 4 + 5 + 6 + 7 + 8 = 33
Blue	8 + 1 + 2 + 9 + 9 + 4 = 33

Green wins!

LOCKER LOGIC (page 6)
A. 10 Left
B. 5 Right
C. 27 Left
D. 16 Right
E. 4 Left
F. 15 Right

SWING SHIFT (page 7)
2:00 p.m. They will finish swinging at 2:10.

HORSING AROUND (pages 8-9)
Even Steven: WHAT DO YOU CALL A PINK PALOMINO?
Odd Rod: A HORSE OF A DIFFERENT COLOR

KEY CLUES (page 10)
1. biT
2. Boot
3. bUg
4. Surf
5. Mouse
6. Ram
7. vIrus
8. chIp
9. Windows
10. wEb
11. meNu
12. screen

All these words are computer terms.

DOTS A LOT (page 11)

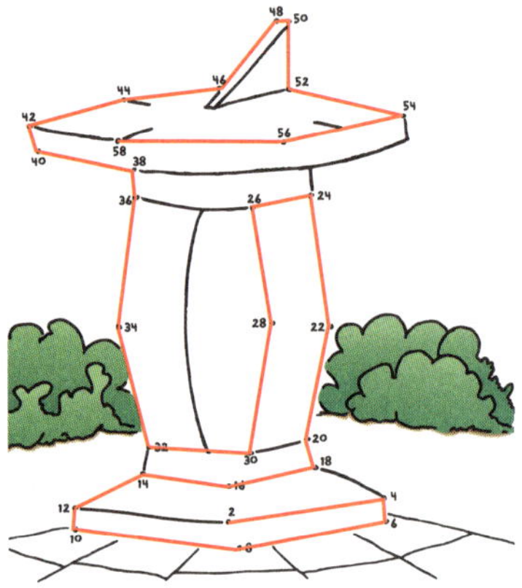

FLIGHT TIMES (pages 12-13)
1. 1
2. 222
3. 11:45 a.m.
4. 5 minutes
5. 7
6. Flight 1402 from Tokyo will come in on time.
7. Two flights: 315 from New York and 8 from Athens
8. Flight 529 from Rio de Janeiro is late by 11 hours.
9. Flight 511 from Dublin will be only five minutes late.
10. Flight 8 from Athens
11. 15 minutes

STACKING STANLEY (page 14)

THINK ABOUT IT (page 15)
1. One (none)
2. Eight (ate)
3. They heard 7 8 9 (seven ate nine).
4. Four

CARNIVAL CLUES (pages 16-17)

Antonia: Roller coaster, 4 times
Beryl: Teacups, 3 times
Delia: Fun house, 8 times
Carlos: Ferris wheel, 7 times
Edward: Train, 6 times

COUNTING PLACES (page 18)

sierra leONE—ONE
sOUth aFRica—FOUR
argENTina—TEN
bENIN—NINE
bOTsWana—TWO
boSnia and hErzEgoViNa—SEVEN
THe GrEnadInes—EIGHT
(THREE appears here as well)

FAST TIMES (page 19)

A. Any number times 0 is 0. All the other numbers don't count at all.
B. Any number times 1 is that number, no matter how big it is. So the answer is still 6,718,923.
C. Any number times 2 is doubled. So in this case, the 5 becomes a 10. The answer is 10,000,000.

CROSSNUMBER (pages 20-21)

[1] 1	[2] 4	9	[3] 2	■	[4] 1	[5] 3
[6] 1	0	■	[7] 0	[8] 2	1	0
1	■	[9] 1	0	0	0	■
[10] 2	[11] 5	■	0	■	[12] 3	[13] 1
■	[14] 1	[15] 9	0	0	■	9
[16] 1	9	9	0	■	[17] 4	0
[18] 3	0	■	[19] 0	2	5	3

THREE BEES (page 22)

ONE	TWO	THREE
FIRST	SECOND	THIRD
PRIMARY	SECONDARY	TERTIARY

MAIL RUN (page 23)

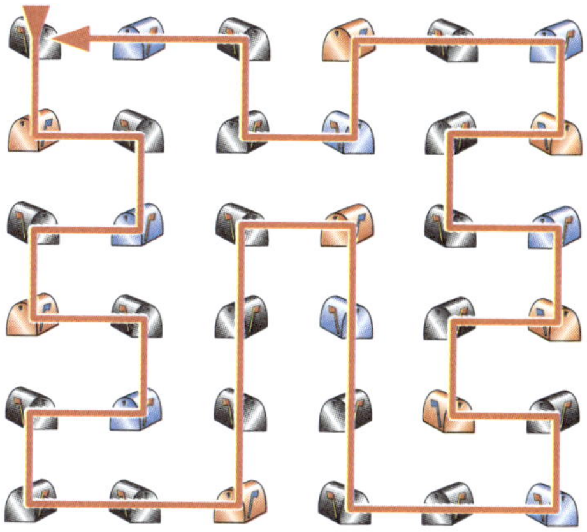

DIGIT DOES IT (pages 24-25)

Dear Inspector Digit,
Your dog knocked over my apiaries! My bees were hiveless. A few workers are still missing. I won't drone on, but would like your help to find my last 23 bees.
Honey B. Bumble

a-2	e-6	i-10	n-14	s-18	w-1
b-3	f-7	k-11	o-15	t-19	y-22
c-4	g-8	l-12	p-16	u-20	
d-5	h-9	m-13	r-17	v-21	

SCRAMBLED PICTURE (pages 26-27)

JUST A SECOND (page 28)

1. second base
2. second best
3. second chance
4. second cousin
5. second-degree
6. second fiddle
7. second floor
8. second-guess
9. secondhand
10. second nature
11. second opinion
12. second sight
13. second thought
14. second wind

FAMILY LOGIC (page 29)

1. Nine: seven boys and two girls. Each brother has the same two sisters.
2. Seven. Each red-haired child has three red-haired siblings and three brown-haired ones. Each brown-haired child has two brown-haired siblings and four red-haired siblings.

PIPELINES (pages 30-31)

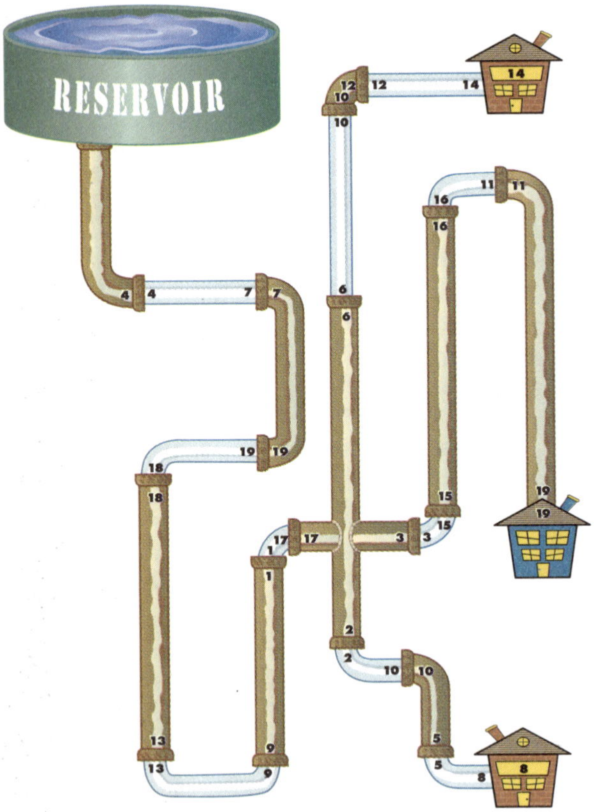

MATHMAGIC (page 32)

The answer is always 13. Try it on your friends.

SAND ART (page 33)

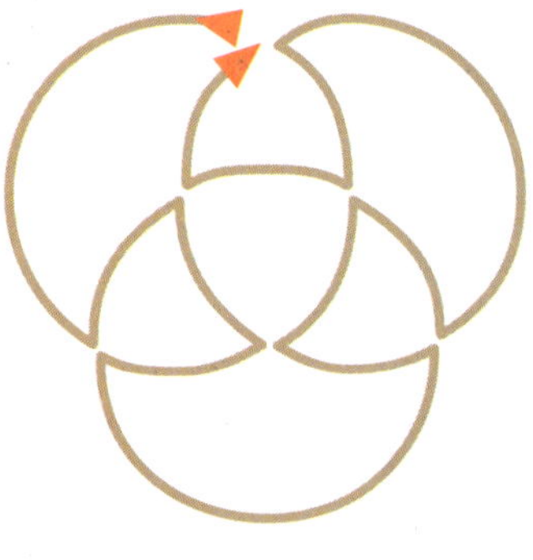

TO A DISTANT PLANET (pages 34-35)

Daring—12,000 miles
Quixocort—10,000 miles (or 52,800,000 feet)
Baxter—20,000 miles (or 32,186 kilometers)
Conn—11,000 miles (or 19,360,000 yards)
Capt. Bruce Baxter has the longest flight.

LIBRARY LAUGHS (page 36)

5 + 3 = 8	H	8 – 6 = 2	B
3 × 5 = 15	O	5 × 5 = 25	Y
29 – 6 = 23	W	36 ÷ 2 = 18	R
27 ÷ 3 = 9	I	12 – 11 = 1	A
4 + 3 = 7	G	8 + 6 = 14	N
7 ÷ 7 = 1	A	12 ÷ 3 = 4	D
24 – 4 = 20	T	5 × 5 = 25	Y
4 × 2 = 8	H	14 + 6 = 20	T
3 + 2 = 5	E	2 × 9 = 18	R
27 – 9 = 18	R	9 – 8 = 1	A
40 ÷ 8 = 5	E	45 ÷ 15 = 3	C
2 × 2 = 4	D	14 + 6 = 20	T
9 ÷ 3 = 3	C	29 – 14 = 15	O
6 × 3 = 18	R	11 + 7 = 18	R
18 – 3 = 15	O		
13 + 3 = 16	P		
16 + 3 = 19	S		

HOW I GATHERED CROPS
by Randy Tractor

PIE TIME (page 37)

A. $\frac{2}{3}$ $\frac{1}{6}$ $\frac{1}{6}$

B. $\frac{2}{5}$ $\frac{2}{5}$ $\frac{1}{5}$

C. $\frac{1}{2}$ $\frac{1}{4}$ $\frac{1}{4}$

HOWARD'S HOUSE (pages 38-39)